Teach Me...™
Korean
and
More Korean

by Judy Mahoney

D1709888

Teach Me Korean and More Korean
Two books in one, twice the fun!
39 songs to sing and learn Korean

The classic coloring books *Teach Me Korean* and *Teach Me More Korean* are now combined into a new bind up edition. This new edition includes the original coloring pages from both titles with a 60 minute audio CD. *Teach Me Korean* and *More Korean* also features six new pages of expanded vocabulary and activities.

Our mission at Teach Me Tapes is to enrich children through language learning. The *Teach Me...*series of books offers an engaging approach to language acquisition by using familiar children's songs and providing an audio to sing and learn. Studies show that a child's early exposure to new languages and cultures enhances learning skills and promotes a better appreciation of our multicultural world. We believe it is important for children to listen, speak, read and write the language to enhance the learning experience. What better gift to offer our youth than the tools and ideas to understand the world we live in?

All Koreans speak and write the same language. Koreans have developed several different dialects in addition to the standard used in Seoul. The dialects, except for that of Jeju-do province, are similar enough for native speakers to understand without any difficulty. Koreans use their own unique alphabet called Hangul, which consists of 10 vowels and 14 consonants. It can be combined to form numerous syllabic groupings. Korean words are usually spelled as they sound.

Today's "global children" hold tomorrow's world in their hands!

Teach Me Korean & More Korean
Bind Up Edition
Book with CD
ISBN: 978-1-59972-610-6
Library of Congress Control Number: 2009901062

Copyright © 2009 Teach Me Tapes, Inc.
6016 Blue Circle Drive
Minnetonka, MN 55343-9104
1-800-456-4656
www.teachmetapes.com

Translations are not literal.

Printed in the United States of America
10 9 8 7 6 5 4 3 2

Teach me...
KOREAN

A Musical
Journey
Through
the Day

by
Judy Mahoney

Teach Me...™

www.teachmetapes.com

 다같이

우리 모두 다같이 즐겁게 노래해

우리 모두 다같이 노래하자

너의 친구 나의 친구

나의 친구 너의 친구

우리 모두 다같이 즐거웁게

안녕하세요, 저의 이름은 영희에요.
여러분의 이름은 무엇이에요?
우리 가족이에요.

아버지

어머니

나

동생 철수

고양이

고양이 이름은 야옹이에요.
회색의 부드러운 털을 가지고 있지요.

강아지

강아지 이름은 바둑이에요.
흰색에 검정 얼룩이 있지요.

이것이 우리 집이에요. 푸른색에 갈색 지붕이 있고,
노란색 꽃들이 가득한 정원이 있어요.

저의 방은 빨간색이에요.
7시에요.
일어나요! 일어나!

 둥근해가 떴습니다

둥근 해가 떴습니다 자리에서 일어나서
제일 먼저 이를 닦자 윗니 아랫니 닦자
세수할 때는 깨끗이 이쪽 저쪽 목 닦고
머리 빗고 옷을 입고 거울을 봅니다
꼭꼭 씹어 밥을 먹고 가방 메고 인사하고
유치원에 갑니다 씩씩하게 갑니다

 강아지

우리집 강아지는 복슬 강아지
어머니가 빨래 가면 멍멍멍
쫄랑쫄랑 따라가며 멍멍멍
우리집 강아지는 예쁜 강아지
학교 갔다 돌아오면 멍멍멍
꼬리치고 반갑다고 멍멍멍

옷을 입어요.
윗도리를 입고,

바지를 입고,

신발을 신고,

모자를 써요.

아침식사때,
저는 시리얼과
잼을 바른 토스트를 먹고,
오랜지 쥬스를 마시는것을
좋아해요.

5 오

머리 어깨 무릎 발

♪

머리 어깨 무릎 발 무릎 발
머리 어깨 무릎 발 무릎 발
머리 어깨 발 무릎 발
머리 어깨 무릎 귀 코 입

오늘은 월요일이에요!
여러분은 요일을 알아요?

월요일

화요일

수요일

목요일

금요일

토요일

일요일

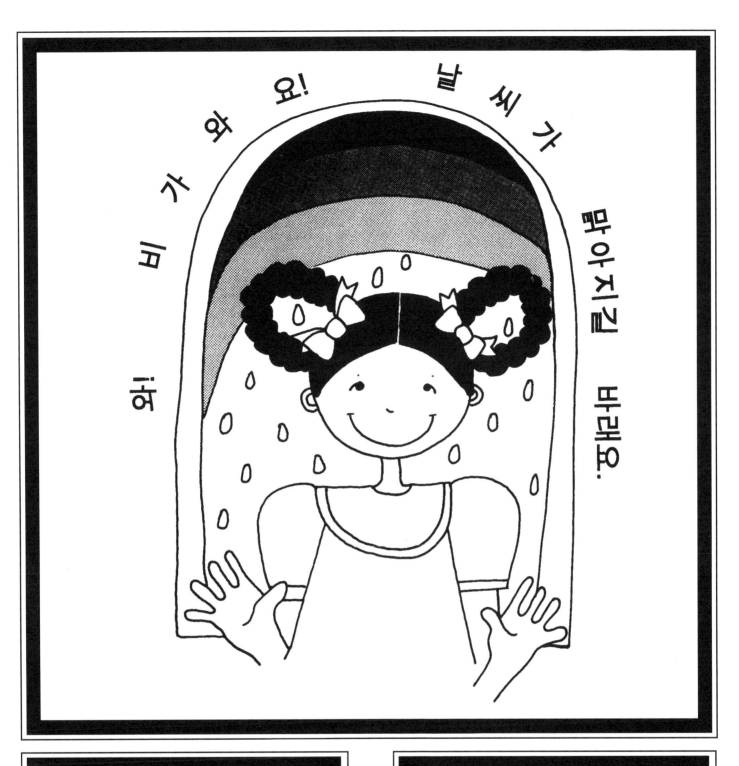

비가 와요! 날씨가 맑아지길 바래요. 해

♪ 구슬비
송알송알 싸리잎에 은구슬
조롱조롱 거미줄에 옥구슬
대롱대롱 풀잎마다 총총총
방긋 웃는 꽃잎마다 송송송
고이고이 오색실에 꿰어서
달빛 새는 창문가에 두라고
포슬포슬 구슬비는 종일
예쁜 구슬 맺히면서 술술술

♪ 우산
이슬비 내리는 이른 아침에
우산 셋이 나란히 걸어갑니다
파란 우산 깜장 우산 찢어진 우산
좁다란 학교길에 우산 세개가
이마를 마주대고 걸어갑니다

하나 둘 셋 넷 다섯
여섯 일곱 여덟 아홉 열

여기가 저의 학교에요.
오늘 저는 숫자와 한글을 반복해서 공부할거에요.
저랑 같이 해보시겠어요?

열 꼬마 인디안

한 꼬마 두 꼬마 세 꼬마 인디안

네 꼬마 다섯 꼬마 여섯 꼬마 인디안

일곱 꼬마 여덟 꼬마 아홉 꼬마 인디안

열 꼬마 인디안 보이

코끼리 한 마리

코끼리 한 마리가 거미줄에 걸렸네
신나게 그네를 탔다네
너무 너무 재밌어
다른 친구 코끼리도 또 불렀네.

코끼리 두 마리가 거미줄에 걸렸네
신나게 그네를 탔다네
너무 너무 재밌어
다른 친구 코끼리도 또 불렀네.

코끼리 세 마리가 ...
코끼리 네 마리가 ...
코끼리 다섯 마리가 ...
코끼리 여섯 마리가 ...
코끼리 일곱 마리가 ...
코끼리 여덟 마리가 ...
코끼리 아홉 마리가 ...
코끼리 열 마리가 ...

우리 모두 다같이

우리 모두 다같이 손뼉을 (짝짝)
우리 모두 다같이 손뼉을 (짝짝)
우리 모두 다같이 즐거웁게 노래해
우리 모두 다같이 손뼉을 (짝짝)

우리 모두 다같이 발 굴러 (쿵쿵)
우리 모두 다같이 발 굴러 (쿵쿵)
우리 모두 다같이 즐거웁게 노래해
우리 모두 다같이 발 굴러 (쿵쿵)

둥글게 둥글게

둥글게 둥글게 (손뼉) 둥글게 둥글게 (손뼉)
빙글빙글 돌아가며 춤을 춥시다 (손뼉)
손뼉을 치면서 (손뼉) 노래를 부르며 (손뼉)
랄랄랄라 즐겁게 춤추자
링가링가 링가 링가링가링 (2X)
손에 손을 잡고 모두 다함께 즐겁게 뛰어봅시다
둥글게 둥글게 (손뼉) 둥글게 둥글게 (손뼉)
빙글빙글 돌아가며 춤을 춥시다 (손뼉)
손뼉을 치면서 (손뼉) 노래를 부르며 (손뼉)
랄랄랄라 즐겁게 춤추자

방과후 우리는
차를 타고 집에 가요.

 자동차

자동차의 바퀴가 데굴 데굴 데굴 데굴 데굴 데굴
자동차의 바퀴가 데굴 데굴 동네를 돌며

자동차의 경적소리 빵빵빵 빵빵빵 빵빵빵
자동차의 경적소리 빵빵빵 동네를 돌며

자동차의 어린이가 밥먹자 밥먹자 밥먹자
자동차의 어린이가 밥먹자 동네를 돌며

자동차의 불빛이 반짝 반짝 반짝 반짝 반짝 반짝
자동차의 불빛이 반짝 반짝 동네를 돌며

자동차의 와이퍼가 쉭쉭쉭 쉭쉭쉭 쉭쉭쉭
자동차의 와이퍼가 쉭쉭쉬 동네를 돌며

자동차의 운전수가 밸트메 밸트메 밸트메
자동차의 운전수가 밸트메 동네를 돌며

 꼬마 자동차 붕붕

붕붕붕 아주 작은 자동차 꼬마 자동차가 나간다
붕붕붕 꽃향기를 맡으면 힘이 솟는 꼬마 자동차

엄마 찾아 모험 찾아 낯설은 세계여행
우리도 함께 가지요

꼬마차가 나가신다 길을 비켜라
꼬마차가 나가신다 길을 비켜라
랄랄랄라 랄랄랄라

귀여운 꼬마차가 친구와 함께
어렵고 험한 길 헤쳐나간다
희망과 사랑을 심어주면서 아하
신나게 달린다 귀여운 꼬마 자동차 붕붕

점심 시간이에요. 점심식사후 저는 휴식을 취해요.

♪ 아빠와 크레파스

어제 밤에 우리 아빠가
다정하신 모습으로
한 손에는 크레파스를
사가지고 오셨어요 음음.
그릴 것은 너무 많은데
하얀 종이가 너무 작아서
아빠 얼굴 그리고 나니
잠이 들고 말았어요 음음.
밤새 꿈나라에
아기 코끼리가 춤을 추었고
크레파스 병정들은
나뭇잎을 타고 놀았죠 음음.
어제밤엔 달빛도
아빠의 웃음처럼
나의 창에 기대어
포근히 날 재워줬어요 음음

모두 다 뛰놀자

모두다 흡흡흡 뛰어라. 모두다 훨훨훨 날아라.

모두다 동동동 굴러라. 모두다 빙빙빙 돌아라.

우~ 우~ 와 와 와 와 와. 우~ 우~ 와 와 와 와우 와.

휴식을 취한 후,

저는 공원으로 놀러 가요.

오리에게 먹이주는것을 좋아해요.

저는 친구와 같이 다리위에서

노래하고 춤을 춰요.

 고기잡이

고기를 잡으러 바다로 갈까나

고기를 잡으러 강으로 갈까나

이 병에 가득히 넣어 가지고요

라라라라라 라라라라라 온다야

쏴쏴쏴 쉬쉬쉬 고기를 몰아서

어여쁜 이 병에 가득히 차면은

선생님한테로 가지고 온다야

라라라라라 라라라라라 안녕

배가고파요! 저녁식사 시간인가봐요!

오, 수잔나!

♪

멀고 먼 앨라베마 나의 고향은 그곳
벤조를 메고 나는 너를 찾아 왔노라
오 수잔나 나의 노랠 부르자
멀고 먼 앨라베마 나의 고향은 그곳

잘자, 친구들아!

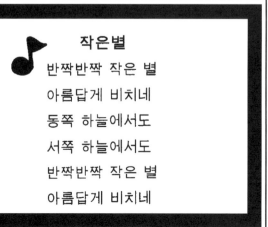

작은별

반짝반짝 작은 별
아름답게 비치네
동쪽 하늘에서도
서쪽 하늘에서도
반짝반짝 작은 별
아름답게 비치네

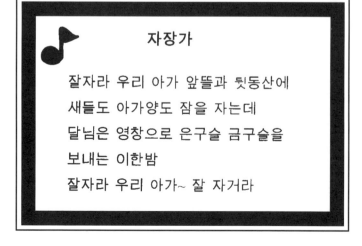

자장가

잘자라 우리 아가 앞뜰과 뒷동산에
새들도 아가양도 잠을 자는데
달님은 영창으로 은구슬 금구슬을
보내는 이한밤
잘자라 우리 아가~ 잘 자거라

Translations

Page 1
The More We Get Together
Let's sing joyfully together
Let's sing together
Your friend, my friend
My friend, your friend
Let's do it joyfully together.

Page 2
Hello, my name is Young-hee.
What is your name?
This is my family: father, mother,
brother Chul-soo, and me.

Page 3
My cat. Her name is Yaong-ee.
She has gray and soft hair.
My dog. His name is Bahdook-ee.
He is white with a block spot.
This is my house. It is blue with a brown
roof and a garden full of yellow flowers.

Page 4
My room is red. It's seven o'clock.
Get up! Get up!

Sun is Up
The round sun rose. Wake up!
First you brush your teeth
Brush the upper and the lower teeth
When you wash your face, wash your neck
This side and that side
Comb your hair, get dressed
And look at the mirror
Eat breakfast, chew thoroughly
Grab your bag, and say good-bye
Go to school. Go briskly.

Our Puppy
Our puppy is a plump and shaggy puppy
When mother goes to do laundry, bow-wow
Following her happily, bow-wow.

Our puppy is a pretty puppy
When I get back from school, bow-wow
Wagging its tail gladly, bow-wow.

Page 5
I get dressed. I put on my shirt, my pants, my
shoes and my hat. For breakfast, I like to eat
cereal, toast with jam and drink orange juice.

Page 6
Head, Shoulders, Knees & Toes
Head, shoulder, knees, toes, knees, toes
Head, shoulder, knees, toes, knees, toes
Head, shoulder, toes, knees, toes
Head, shoulder, knees, mouth, nose, ears.

Page 7
Today is Monday. Do you know the days of
The week? Monday, Tuesday, Wednesday,
Thursday, Friday, Saturday, Sunday.

Page 8
Oh! It's raining! I wish the sun would come
out!

Rain Song
Silver beads hanging on a leaf of clover bush
Dangle-dangle jade bead on the cobweb
Dangle-dangle densely on each leaf
On each smiling petal '*song, song, song*'.

Beautifully, thread the beads on colorful
Strings; put them beside the window
Where the moonlight comes through softly
All day the beaded rain
Forms pretty beads '*sole, sole, sole*'.

Umbrellas
In the early drizzling morning
Three umbrellas are walking side by side
A blue umbrella, a black umbrella
And a ragged umbrella
Three umbrellas on the narrow road to school
Walking closely to each other.

Page 9
Here is my school. Today, I will repeat the
numbers and Korean alphabet. Will you say
them with me? One, two, three, four, five, six,
seven, eight, nine, ten. Yeah!

Korean alphabet:
ㄱ*(gi-yeok)*, ㄴ*(ni-eun)*, ㄷ*(di-geut)*,
ㄹ*(li-eul)*, ㅁ*(mi-eum)*, ㅂ*(bi-eub)*,
ㅅ*(si-yot)*, ㅇ*(i-eung)*, ㅈ*(ji-eut)*,
ㅊ*(chi-eut)*, ㅋ*(ki-eok)*, ㅌ*(ti-geut)*,
ㅍ*(pi-eub)*, ㅎ*(hi-eut)*
ㅏ*(a)*, ㅑ*(ya)*, ㅓ*(eo)*, ㅕ*(yeo)*, ㅗ*(o)*,
ㅛ*(yo)*, ㅜ*(u)*, ㅠ*(yu)*, ㅡ*(eu)*, ㅣ*(i)*

Translations

Page 10
Ten Little Indians
One little two little three little Indians
Four little five little six little Indians
Seven little eight little nine little Indians
Ten little Indian boys.

One Elephant
One elephant upon a spider's web
He swung joyfully
He had such enormous fun
That he called for another elephant to come.

Two elephants upon a spider's web
They swung joyfully
They had such enormous fun
That they called for another elephant to come.

Three elephants…four…five…six…
Seven…eight…nine…ten

If You're Happy & You Know It
Let's all together clap hands (clap, clap)
Let's all together clap hands (clap, clap)
Let's all together sing a song happily
Let's all together clap hands. (clap, clap)

Let's all together stomp feet (stomp, stomp)
Let's all together stomp feet (stomp, stomp)
Let's all together sing a song happily
Let's all together stomp feet. (stomp, stomp)

Let's all together laugh out loud (giggle)
Let's all together laugh out loud (giggle)
Let's all together sing a song happily
Let's all together laugh out loud. (giggle)

Let's all together, deliciously (mm, mm)
Let's all together, deliciously (mm, mm)
Let's all together sing a song happily
Let's all together, deliciously. (mm, mm)

Let's all together take a nap (hoo)
Let's all together take a nap (hoo)
Let's all together sing a song happily
Let's all together take a nap. (hoo)

Round, Round
Round, round (clap)
Round, round (clap)
Round, round, turn around
And dance together. (clap)

Clap your hands (clap)
Sing together (clap)
Lahl laha lahl la
Let's dance joyfully.

Ring-gah ring-gah ring~gah
Ring-gah ring-gah ring
Ring-gah ring-gah ring
Hand in hand
Let's dance together joyfully.

Round, round (clap)
Round, round (clap)
Round, round, turn around
And dance together (clap)

Clap your hands (clap)
Sing together (clap)
Lahl laha lahl la
Let's dance joyfully.

Page 11
After school, we ride home in the car.

The Wheels on the Car
The wheels on the car go round and round
Round and round, round and round
The wheels on the car go round and round
All around the town.

The horn on the car goes beep beep beep
Beep beep beep, beep beep beep
The horn on the car goes beep beep beep
All around the town.

The children in the car go, "Let's have lunch"
"Let's have lunch, let's have lunch"
The children in the car go, "Let's have lunch"
All around the town.

Translations

Little Car *Boong Boong*
Boong Boong Boong, a tiny car
The little car on its way
Boong Boong Boong, it smells the flowers
Which give the little car its strength
Looking for mom and adventure
Unfamiliar world, we are going together.

The little car on its way, get out of the way!
The little car on its way, get out of the way!
Lahl lahl lahl lah, lahl lahl lahl lah.

The cute little car with its friend
Go through the rough and hard road
Giving hope and love (ah-ha)
Running happily.
The cute little car, *Boong Boong*.
© Hyung-shin Park, 1986

Page 12
It is time for lunch. After lunch, I take a quiet time.

Dad and the Crayon
Last night, my dad, with a loving look
He bought a crayon
And gave it to me (mm, mm)
There were lots of things to draw
But the white paper was too small
I fell asleep after I finished
Drawing my dad's face (mm, mm)
All night, in the dreamland
A baby elephant was dancing
And crayon soldiers
Were riding leaves (mm, mm)
Last night's moonlight
Warm like my dad's smile
Leaned on my window
Waiting for me to sleep.
© Hyae-min Lee

Page 13
After my quiet time, I go to the park to play. I like to feed the ducks. I sing and dance on the bridge with my friends.

Let's Play Together
Everybody *hop-hop-hop* jump
Everybody *hirr-hirr-hirr* fly
Everybody *dong-dong-dong* stamp
Everybody *bing-bing-bing* turn
Woo-woo-wha wha wha wha wha. (2X)

Let's Go Fishing
Let's go to the ocean to fish
Let's go to the river to fish
Fill up this bottle
La la la la, la la la la, come back.

Sha sha sha, shi shi shi, trapping fish
When this pretty bottle is full
Take it to our teacher
La la la la, la la la la, good-bye.

Page 14
I'm hungry! It must be time for dinner.

Oh! Susanna
Far faraway Alabama, that's my hometown
Carrying a banjo, I came to visit you
Oh, Susanna! Let's sing my song
Far faraway Alabama, that's my hometown.

Page 15
It's nighttime. Do you see the stars?
Goodnight, Mom. Goodnight, Dad. I love you.

Twinkle, Twinkle Little Star
Twinkle, twinkle little star
Lighting beautifully
In the east sky
In the west sky
Twinkle, twinkle little star
It shines beautifully.

Lullaby
Sleep well, my baby
In the garden and on the back hill
Birds and lambs are sleeping
The moon brings silver
And gold beads to the dawn
Through the night
Sleep well, my baby. Sleep well.

Goodnight, My Friends
Goodnight, my friends, goodnight
Goodnight, my friends, goodnight
Goodnight, my friends
Goodnight, my friends
Goodnight, my friends, goodnight
Goodnight!

Translated by Cheon Hee Lee
With special help from: Hae Jin Hong,
Jung Eun Yi and Joo Yun Lee

NOTES

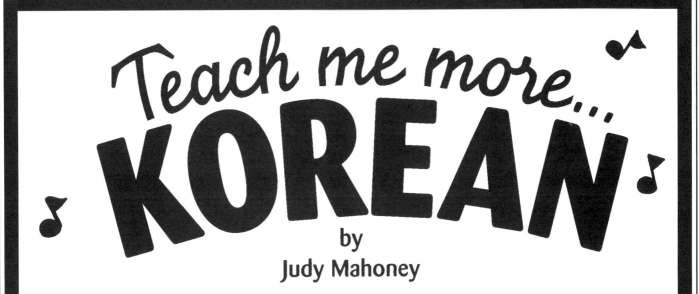

KOREAN

by
Judy Mahoney

A Musical Journey Through the Year

Learn Korean the fun way!

Teach Me...™
www.teachmetapes.com

매리: 안녕하세요. 제 이름은 매리에요. 제 동생이에요. 동생
 이름은 피터에요. 우리는 강아지를 가지고 있어요. 강아지
 이름은 스팟이에요. 우리는 고양이를 가지고 있어요. 고양이
 이름은 플러피에요. 한 해를 저희와 함께 여행해 봐요.

다같이 노래 부르자
노래 부르자 노래 부르자. 우리 모두 다같이 노래 부르자.
노래 부르자 노래 부르자. 봄 여름 가을 겨울.

Music by Ella Jenkins, ASCAP. Copyright 1996 Ell-Bern Publishing Co. Used by permission.

피터: 봄이에요. 전 정원을 가꿔요. 하얗고 노란 제 데이지
　　　꽃을 보세요!

매리: 저는 과일과 채소를 가꾸기 위해 저의 정원에 씨를
　　　뿌려요. 올해에는 딸기, 토마토, 당근, 배추, 그리고
　　　호박을 가꿀 거에요.

밀과 콩과 보리
밀과 보리가 자란다.

꽃밭에서
아빠하고 나하고 만든 꽃밭에
채송화도 봉숭아도 한창입니다
아빠가 매어놓은 새끼줄 따라
나팔꽃도 어울리게 피었습니다.
(Complete verses appear on page 16)

동물원에 가요
내일 동물원에 함께 가요.
엄마와 함께, 엄마와 함께
내일 동물원에 함께 가요.
즐거운 하루

후렴(Chorus):
우린 동물원에 가지요.
여러분은 어때요, 함께 갈래요.
동물원에 가지요.

나무에 매달린 원숭이를 봐요.
...
물속에서 수영하는 악어를 봐요.
...

매리: 오늘 저희는 동물원에 갈 거에요.
사자, 기린, 그리고 원숭이를 보세요.
피터: 동물원에서 제가 가장 좋아하는
동물은 악어에요.

팅갈래요
팅갈래요 작은 당나귀
팅갈래요 작은 당나귀
어쩔땐 빠르고 어쩔땐 늦지만
그래도 언제나 어여쁜 내 당나귀

매리: 제 생일은 5월 5일 이에요. 어린이날 이기도 하지요.
　　　친구들과 함께 파티를 해요. 저의 어머니께서 저를 위해서
　　　크고 둥근 케잌을 만들어 주세요.
피터: 이제 "사이몬이 말하길" 을 할 시간이에요!

♪

생일 축하 노래

생일 축하합니다!

"사이몬이 말하길"

사이몬이 말하길:..."오른손을 머리위에 올려."

...“땅을 짚어.”

...“걸어.”

...“박수쳐.”

...“이름을 말해.”

“크게 웃어.” “사이몬이 말하지 않았는데!”

피터: 봄 다음엔 여름이에요. 여름에는 우리는 해변 가를
   가요. 저는 비치 볼과 장난감 배를 가져가지요.

매리: 저는 모래 양동이와 모래 삽을 해변가로 가져가요.

피터: 저희는 수영복을 입고 큰 모래성을 만들어요.

매리: 스팟, 부수지마.

초록바다

초록빛 바닷물에 두손을 담그면	초록빛 여울물에 (초록빛)
초록빛 바닷물에 두손을 담그면	두발을 담그면 (담그면)
파란 하늘빛 물이 들지요	물결이 살랑 어루만져요
어여쁜 초록빛 손이 되지요	물결이 살랑 어루만져요

매리: 수영을 한 후, 저희는 점심을 먹어요. 저희는 김밥, 당근
그리고 바나나를 먹어요. 맛있어요!

피터: 안돼! 개미들 좀 봐!

매리: 점심식사 후, 저희는 산책을 하죠.

햇볕은 쨍쨍

햇볕은 쨍쨍 모래알은 반짝 모래알로 떡 해놓고 조약돌로 소반지어 언니 누나 모셔다가 맛있게도 얌얌	햇볕은 쨍쨍 모래알은 반짝 호미들고 괭이 매고 뻗어가는 매를 깨어 엄마, 아빠 모셔다가 맛있게도 얌얌

매리: 오늘 저희는 자연역사 박물관을 가요.
피터: 거기엔 공룡들이 많이 있기 때문에 제가 좋아하는
      곳이에요. 트리케라톱스를 보세요. 머리에 세 개의 뿔
      이 있어요.

매리: 다음으로, 저희는 미술 박물관에
　　가기 위해 길을 건너요.
피터: 고야의 그림에 있는 황소를
　　보는걸 좋아해요. 제가 투우사가
　　되는 것을 상상하곤 하죠.
매리: 반 고흐의 그림을 보세요. 그의
　　그림에 있는 꽃이 제 정원에 있는
　　꽃이랑 비슷해요.

귀여운 소녀
동그라미 안에 있어요.
트랄라 랄랄라 [반복 (repeat)]

예쁘고 귀여운 소녀가

2. 움직여 주세요. ...
3. 바다를 건너요. ...
4. 춤을 추어주세요. ...

매리: 여름 다음에는 가을이에요. 나뭇잎들이 노란색, 빨간색,
　　　주황색으로 물들죠. 저희는 나무에서 떨어진 낙엽과 밤,
　　　도토리 등을 모아요.

산골짜기 다람쥐
산골짝에 다람쥐, 아기 다람쥐.
도토리 점심 가지고 소풍을 간다.
다람쥐야, 다람쥐야, 재주나 한번 넘으렴.
파알딱, 팔딱, 팔딱. 날도 참말 좋구나.

피터: 방학이 끝나기 전에, 저희는
　　　할아버지 농장에 가요. 우리는
　　　소, 닭, 돼지에게 먹이를 주어요.
매리: 할아버지께서는 양털을 깎으세요.
　　　그 다음에, 할아버지께서 사촌들과
　　　저희를 데리고 소풍을 가시지요.

동물농장
1. 닭장 속에는 암닭이 (꼭꼭꼭)
문간 옆에는 거위가 (꺼엉 꺼엉)
배나무 밑엔 염소가 (메~ 메~)
외양간에는 송아지 (음메~)

닭장 속에는 암닭들이 (꼬꼬댁)
문간 옆에는 거위들이 (꺼엉)
배나무 밑엔 염소들이 (메~)
외양간에는 송아지 (음메~)
(X 2)
우와야 우~ 우~ 우~ (X 2)

2. 깊은 산속엔 뻐꾸기 (뻐꾹 뻐꾹)
높은 하늘엔 종달새 (짹짹짹)
부뚜막 위엔 고양이 (야옹 야옹)
마루 밑에는 강아지 (멍 멍)

깊은 산속엔 뻐꾸기가 (뻐꾹 뻐꾹)
높은 하늘엔 종달새가 (짹짹짹)
부뚜막 위엔 고양이가 (야옹 야옹)
마루 밑에는 강아지 (멍 멍)
우와야 우~ 우~ 우~ (X 2)

할아버지 농장으로
우리는 가요 우리는 가요
할아버지 농장으로
즐겁게 함께 할아버지 농장으로 *(반복)*
할아버지네 농장엔 소가 있어요. *(반복)*
그 소는 이렇게 울어요: 음메~ *(반복)*
할아버지네 농장엔 닭이 있어요. *(반복)*
그 닭은 이렇게 울어요: 꼬꼬댁~ *(반복)*

매리: 오늘은 학교에서 운동회가 있는 날이에요. 청팀과 백팀으로
　　　나누어 달리기를 하고, 오재미 던지기를 해요.
피터: 저는 줄다리기와 장애물 달리기를 좋아해요
매리: 저희 부모님도 같이 하지요. 저는 학교 운동회를 제일
　　　좋아해요.

피터: 미국에 사는 사촌이 편지를 보냈어요. 미국에는 할로윈이란 날이 있는데요. 그날에는 큰 주황색 호박을 깎아서 등불을 만든다고 해요.

매리: 우리 모두 할로윈 변장을 해요. 나는 팬다, 피터는 카우보이, 그리고 우리 강아지는 늑대 변장을 해요.

호박 오형제

호박 오형제가 문 앞에 앉아 있습니다.
첫째가 말하길, "오 이런, 늦어지고 있는데."
둘째가 말하길, "저기 하늘에 마녀들이 오고 있어."
셋째가 말하길, "하지만 우린 상관없어."
넷째가 말하길, "서둘러 가자."
다섯째가 말하길, "난 즐길 준비가 되었어."
"휙-익," 바람이 불고 불이 꺼졌습니다.
그리고 호박 오형제는 떠났습니다.

꼬마 눈사람

한겨울에 밀짚모자 꼬마눈사람
눈썹이 우습구나 코도 삐뚤고
거울을 보여줄까 꼬마눈사람
하루종일 우두커니 꼬마눈사람
무엇을 생각하고 혼자 섰느냐
집으로 들여갈까 꼬마눈사람

피터: 봐요, 눈이 내려요. 놀러 나가요.
　　저희는 **썰매**를 가지고 언덕에서
　　썰매를 타요.
매리: 그리고 나서, 저희는 큰 눈사람을
　　만들어요. 눈사람은 숯으로 된 눈,
　　당근 코, 그리고 검은 모자를
　　가지고 있어요. 그리고 눈사람은
　　저의 어머니의 목도리를 하고
　　있어요.

고요한 밤 거룩한 밤

고요한 밤 거룩한 밤 어둠에 묻힌 밤
주의 부모 앉아서 감사기도 드릴 때
아기 잘도 잔다 아기 잘도 잔다

매리: **휴**일이에요. 저희는 크리스마스를 기념해요. 저희는 쿠키를 굽고 저희 집을 꾸며요. 저희는 크리스마스 케롤을 불러요.

피터: 일월 일일은 새해가 시작하는 날이에요. 저희는 새해 전날에 새해를 기념하기 위해 파티를 해요.

설

까치까치 설날은 어저께고요
우리우리 설날은 오늘이래요
곱고고운 댕기도 내가돌이고
새로사온 신발도 내가신어요.

(Complete verses appear on page 16.)

우리언니 저고리 노랑저고리
우리 동생 저고리 색동저고리
아버지와 어머니 호사내시고
우리들의 절받기 좋아하셔요.

매리: 올해 이월에는 정월 대보름이 있어요. 재미있어요.
　　　달맞이를 하고 콩과 오곡밥을 먹어요. 저희는 한복을
　　　입고 친구들과 노래하고 춤을 춰요. 이제 일년동안에
　　　있는 한해의 달을 어떻게 부르는지 알죠? 일월, 이월,
　　　삼월, 사월, 오월, 유월, 칠월, 팔월, 구월, 시월, 십일월,
　　　십이월. 안녕!

매리: 여러분, 즐거운 시간이 됐나요? 다시 한번 들어보세요. 안녕!

Translations

Page 1
You'll Sing a Song
You'll sing a song and I'll sing a song,
And we'll sing a song together.
You'll sing a song and I'll sing a song,
In warm or wintry weather.
Words and music by Ella Jenkins. ASCAP
Copyright 1966. Ell-Bern Publishing Co. Used by permission.

*MARIE: Hello, My name is Marie. This is my
brother. His name is Peter. We have a dog.
His name is Spot. We have a cat. Her name is
Fluffy. Follow us through the year.*

Page 2 MARCH
*PETER: It is spring. I plant a flower garden.
Look at my white and yellow daisies!
MARIE: I plant seeds to grow fruit and
vegetables in my garden. This year, I will
grow strawberries, tomatoes, carrots,
cabbage and pumpkins.*

Oats & Beans & Barley
Oats and beans and barley grow,
Oats and beans and barley grow.
Do you or I or anyone know
How oats and beans and barley grow?

First the farmer plants the seeds,
Stands up tall and takes his ease,
Stamps his feet and claps his hands
And turns around to view his land.

Then the farmer waters the ground,
Watches the sun shine all around,
Stamps his feet and claps his hands
And turns around to view his land.

In the Flower Garden
In the garden that my dad and I made,
The moss roses and balsams are at their best.
Following the straw rope tied by my dad,
The morning glory bloomed well.

While playing with friends,
I missed my father, so I looked at a flower.
Dad said to me, let's live looking at flowers.
Dad said to me that life is like flowers.

Page 3 APRIL
*MARIE: Today we will go to the zoo. Look at
the lion, the giraffe and the monkey.
PETER: My favorite animal at the zoo is the
crocodile.*

Going to the Zoo
Momma's (Daddy's) taking us
To the zoo tomorrow,
Zoo tomorrow, zoo tomorrow,

Momma's (Daddy's) taking us
To the zoo tomorrow, we can stay all day.

Chorus:
We're going to the zoo, zoo, zoo
How about you, you, you?
You can come too, too, too
We're going to the zoo, zoo, zoo.

2. Look at all the monkeys swingin'* in the
trees…

3. Look at all the crocodiles swimmin'** in
the water…
Word & music by Tom Paxton. Copyright 1961, renewed 1989.
Cherry Lane Music Publishing Co., Inc. All rights reserved.
Used by permission.

* "swingin'" is slang for "swinging."
** "swimmin'" is slang for "swimming."

Tingalayo
Tingalayo, come little donkey come.
Tingalayo, come little donkey come.
Me donkey fast, me*** donkey slow,
Me donkey come and me donkey go.
Me donkey fast, me donkey slow,
Me donkey come and me donkey go.

*** "me" is slang for "my."

Page 4 MAY
Happy Birthday
Happy birthday to you!

*MARIE: My birthday is May 5th. It is
Children's Day. I have a party with my
friends. My mother bakes me a big, round
cake.
PETER: OK. Now it's time to play "Simon
Says!"*

Simon Says
Simon says: … "put your right hand
on your head."
… "touch the ground."
… "walk."
… "clap your hands."
… "say your name."
"Marie, Peter, Jenny, Joey."
"Laugh out loud." "Simon didn't say!"

Page 5 JUNE
*PETER: After spring, it is summer. In the
summer, we go to the beach. I bring my beach
ball and toy boat.*

16 십육

MARIE: I bring my sand pail and shovel to the beach.
PETER: We put on our swimsuits and build huge castles in the sand.
MARIE: Spot, don't knock it down!

Green Ocean
When you dip your hands in the green ocean
When you dip your hands in the green ocean
They will be like the sky.
They will be pretty green hands.
In green ocean (green).
When you dip your feet (dip)
The water passes over feet smoothly.
The water passes over feet smoothly.

Page 6 JULY
MARIE: After we swim, we eat our picnic lunch. We eat kimbop (Korean sushi), carrots, and bananas. It is delicious!
PETER: Oh no! Look at the ants!
MARIE: After having lunch, we go for a walk.

Sunshine
Sunshine
The grains of sand twinkling.
Bake rice cakes of the grains of sand.
Cook a meal of small stones.
Invite sisters for the meal.
Eat it yum yum.

Sunshine
The grains of sand twinkling.
Hold a hoe and a mattock
Plow a field.
Invite mom and dad for the meal.
Eat it yum yum.

Page 7 AUGUST
MARIE: Today, we go to the natural history museum.
PETER: It is my favorite place because there are so many dinosaurs. Look at the triceratops. It has three horns on its head.

Page 8 AUGUST
MARIE: Next, we go across the street to visit the art museum.
PETER: I like to look at the bulls in Goya's painting. I pretend I am the matador.
MARIE: Look at the painting by Van Gogh. The flowers in his painting look like the ones in my garden.

Brown Girl in the Ring
Brown girl in the ring,
Tra-la-la-la-la (repeat)
She looks like a sugar
And a plum, plum, plum!

2. Show me a motion…
3. Skip across the ocean…
4. Do the locomotion…

Page 9 SEPTEMBER
MARIE: After summer, it is autumn. The leaves turn gold, red and orange. We gather leaves and acorns that fall from trees.

The Squirrel
In a valley, a squirrel, a baby squirrel.
He goes to a picnic bringing acorns for lunch.
Squirrel, squirrel, does tricks.
Hopping, hopping, hopping. It is a nice day.

Page 10 OCTOBER
PETER: Before we go back to school, we visit Grandpa's farm. We feed the cows, chickens and pigs.
MARIE: Grandpa shears the wool from the sheep. Later, he takes us on a picnic with our cousins.

Down on Grandpa's Farm
Oh, we're on our way, we're on our way
On our way to Grandpa's farm. (repeat)
Down on Grandpa's farm there is a big
Brown cow (repeat)
The cow, she makes a sound like this: Moo! (repeat)
… there is a little red hen (repeat)
The hen, she makes a sound like this: Cluck! Cluck! (repeat)

Animal Farm
1. There is a hen in a henhouse. (cluck cluck)
There is a goose by the doorway. (gung gung)
There is a goat under a pear tree. (me me)
There is a calf in a cowshed. (moo)

There are hens in a henhouse. (cluck cluck)
There are geese by the doorway. (gung gung)
There are goats under a pear tree. (me me)
There are calves in a cowshed. (moo)

Woo-wa-ya woo~ woo~ woo~ (repeat)

2. There is a cuckoo deep in the mountains. (butkuk)
There is a skylark in the sky. (chek chek)
There is a cat on a kitchen range. (yaong yaong)
There is a dog under a wooden floor. (mung mung) (repeat)

Woo-wa-ya woo~ woo~ woo~ (repeat)

Translations

Page 11 OCTOBER

MARIE: Today, we have an athletic festival at school. Students are divided into a blue team and a white team. We run a race and throw a hackey sack.

PETER: I like tug-of-war and an obstacle race.

MARIE: My parents do them together with us. The school athletic festival is my favorite.

Page 12 OCTOBER & NOVEMBER

PETER: My cousin, who lives in the U.S., sent a letter. In the U.S., there is Halloween. On this day, people carve a face on pumpkins.

MARIE: We will dress up in Halloween costumes. I will be a panda, Peter will be a cowboy, and Spot will be the wolf. American kids will go trick-or-treating by going around their town. It sounds fun.

PETER: After Halloween, it is November.

Five Little Pumpkins

Five little pumpkins sitting on a gate
First one said, "Oh my, it's getting late."
Second one said,
"There are witches in the air."
Third one said, "But we don't care."
The fourth one said,
"Let's run and run and run."
The fifth one said, "I'm ready for some fun."
"Oo-oo," went the wind and
Out went the light,
And the five little pumpkins
Rolled out of sight.

Page 13 DECEMBER

PETER: Look, snow is falling. Let's go and play in the snow. We take our sleds and slide down the hill.

MARIE: Then we'll build a huge snowman. He has coal eyes, a carrot nose and a derby hat. He wears my mother's scarf.

Little Snowman

In midwinter, there is a little snowman
With a straw hat.
He has funny eyebrows and a slanting nose.
Do you want to see a mirror, little snowman?
You stand up all day, little snowman.
By yourself, what do you think about?
Do you want to go home, little snowman?

Silent Night

Silent night, holy night
All is calm, all is bright
'Round yon Virgin, Mother and Child,
Holy infant, so tender and mild,
Sleep in heavenly peace. (repeat)

Page 14 DECEMBER & JANUARY

MARIE: It is holiday time. We celebrate Christmas. We bake cookies and decorate our house. We sing Christmas carols.

PETER: January first begins the New Year. We have a party to celebrate on New Year's Eve.

New Year

Korean magpie's New Year was yesterday.
Our New Year is today.
I wear a pretty pigtail ribbon by myself.
I wear new shoes by myself.

My older sister's jacket is a yellow jacket.
My younger sister's jacket is a colorful jacket.
Father and mother are happy.
They like to get a New Year's bow.

In the backyard, we put a seesaw.
We bring a table inside
Peel pine nuts and walnuts.
We play seesaw with my older sister
I'm happy, so happy.

Angry father became nice.
My younger sister doesn't cry.
All houses play the yut game and seesaw.
I like the New Year. I like it so much.

Page 15 FEBRUARY

MARIE: In February, there is New Year Full Moon Day. It is fun. We welcome the first full moon and eat beans and cereal rice. We wear our Hanbok costumes and sing and dance with our friends. Now we know the months of the year. Do you?

Months of the Year

January, February, March, April, May, June, July, August, September, October, November, December.

MARIE: Everyone, did you have a good time? Try to listen again. Good-bye!

Translated by Cheon Hee Lee

With special help from: Hae Jin Hong, Jung Eun Yi and Joo Yun Lee

The Hangul alphabet has 24 letters – 14 consonants and 10 vowels. Korean words are usually spelled as they sound. There are no capital letters. The letters making up each syllable are written together to form a square-shaped character.

A syllable is made up of: consonant + vowel **or** consonant + vowel + consonant

Pronunciation Guide

Many Korean sounds are similar to English, however some require special attention. Please note these pronunciation tips:

人   As *s*, except when followed by *ee*, when it is as *sh*.

ㅎ   As *h*, except at the end of a syllable, when it is *ng* as in 'king'.

ㄹ   As *r* in rain or *l* in lily. After an *m*, *n* or *ng* sound, it is as *n*.

ㅏ   As *a* in 'ah'.

ㅑ   As *ya* in 'yard'.

NOTES

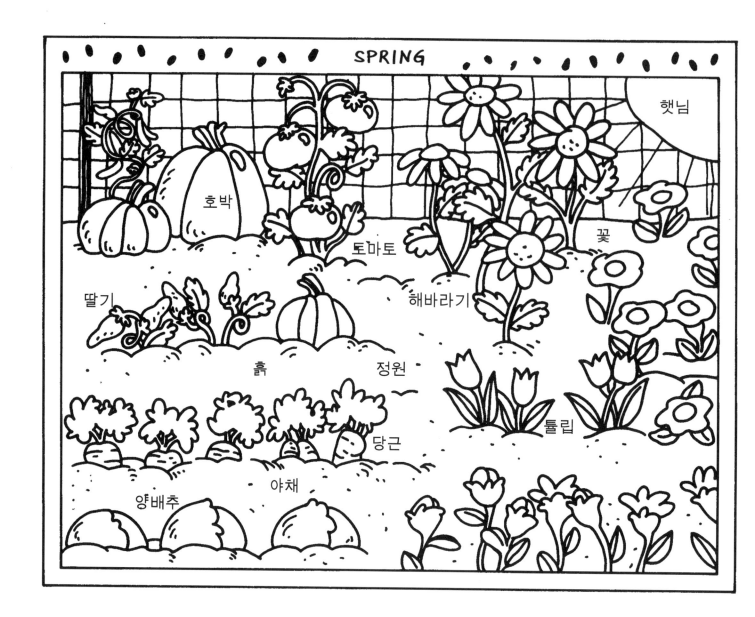

봄
Spring Vocabulary
Find the matching words in the picture.

soil _____   tulip _____

strawberries _____   carrots _____

vegetables _____   flowers _____

pumpkin _____   sunflower _____

cabbage _____   sun _____

tomato _____   garden _____

SUMMER

여름
Summer Vocabulary
Find the matching words in the picture.

clouds _____   thermos _____

lake _____   sunglasses _____

beach _____   swimsuit _____

ant _____   cheese _____

sand _____   shoes _____

blanket _____   shirt _____

banana _____   sandwich _____

sailboat _____   cup _____

AUTUMN

하늘
새
스웨터
고양이
바구니
치마
재킷
개 바지
나무
나뭇잎 도토리

가을
Autumn Vocabulary
Find the matching words in the picture.

sky _____   dog _____

leaves _____   jacket _____

sweater _____ basket _____

cat _____   pants _____

skirt _____   tree _____

acorn _____   bird _____

겨울
Winter Vocabulary
Find the matching words in the picture.

hill _____

jacket _____

ice _____

snowflake _____

sled _____

ice skates _____

snow _____

scarf _____

eyes _____

carrot _____

ANSWER KEY FOR VOCABULARY WORDS

봄 (Spring)

	Translation		Translation
soil	흙	tulip	튤립
strawberries	딸기	carrots	당근
vegetables	야채	flowers	꽃
pumpkin	호박	sunflower	해바라기
cabbage	양배추	sun	햇님
tomato	토마토	garden	정원

여름 (Summer)

	Translation		Translation
clouds	구름	thermos	보온병
lake	호수	sunglasses	선글라스
beach	해변	swimsuit	수영복
ant	개미	cheese	치즈
sand	모래	shoes	신발
blanket	담요	shirt	셔츠
banana	바나나	sandwich	샌드위치
sailboat	돛단배	cup	컵

가을 (Autumn)

	Translation		Translation
sky	하늘	dog	개
leaves	나뭇잎	jacket	재킷
sweater	스웨터	basket	바구니
cat	고양이	pants	바지
skirt	치마	tree	나무
acorn	도토리	bird	새

겨울 (Winter)

	Translation		Translation
hill	언덕	ice skates	스케이트
jacket	재킷	snow	눈
ice	얼음	scarf	목도리
snowflake	눈송이	eyes	눈
sled	썰매	carrot	당근